MUTINY ON THE MOOR

(The story of the Dartmoor Prison Riot of 1932)

By SIMON DELL, MBE, QCB

FOREST PUBLISHING

First published in 2006 by FOREST PUBLISHING, Woodstock, Liverton, Newton Abbot, Devon, TQ12 6JJ

Copyright © Simon P. Dell, MBE, QCB 2006

All rights reserved. No part of this book may be reproduced or transmitted in any form or by any means, electronic or mechanical, including photocopying, recording or by any information storage or retrieval system, without written permission from the copyright holder.

British Library Cataloguing in Publication Data.

A catalogue record for this book is available from the British Library.

ISBN 0 9549089 3 7

Forest Publishing

Design, layout and typeset by:
Simon P. Dell, MBE, QCB

Editorial by:
Mike and Karen Lang

Printed and bound in Great Britain by:
The Printing Press, 21 Clare Place, Coxside, Plymouth, Devon, PL4 0JW

Cover photographs:
Front— Dartmoor Prison entrance gates as seen during the riot.
　　　　　　　　　By kind permission of the Western Morning News
Rear — An aerial view of Princetown village and H M P Dartmoor.
　　　　　　　　　　　　　　　　　　　　　　　　　　　　Author

CONTENTS

Dedication 4

Acknowledgements 4

Foreword 5

Introduction 7

1 The Creation of a Powder Keg 11

2 The Scene is Set 17

3 Sunday 24 January 1932 — The Mutiny 25

4 Reinforcements Make Their Way 35

5 The Mutiny Continues 47

6 Help Arrives 51

7 Order is Restored 59

8 The Aftermath 61

9 The Enquiry 65

10 The Trial 67

Post Script 78

Bibliography 79

The Author 80

DEDICATION

This book is dedicated to the spirit of justice, decency, fair play and self-respect which burns, however dimly, in all men.

ACKNOWLEDGEMENTS

A book like this does not just appear without the help and support of many people. The author's name may appear on the front cover, but grateful thanks are due to numerous contributors, namely:- Laura Worth and David Francis (staff of the Prison Heritage Centre at Princetown), along with Mark Miller for kindly contributing the foreword whilst serving his sentence at Dartmoor Prison. Former prison officer, author and Dartmoor Prison authority Ron Joy for proof-reading my manuscripts and setting me back on the right course again when I historically veered off track! My friend, fellow author and former prison employee Trevor James for the loan of photographs and reference material. The staff of the archives of the London Illustrated News, the Daily Mail, the Western Morning News, the Tavistock Times Gazette and the Evening Herald have been more than generous with their help and assistance with many of their archival photographs. Many individual photographs have been loaned to me by numerous people, including former Princetown residents Rosie Oxenham, Andy and Dot Cribbett, and Dave Andrews. Retired Superintendent Derek Roper, formerly a constable stationed at Princetown, allowed the use of the account by his uncle, George Roper. Thanks to Wendy Braithwaite and Jo Smith for reading and correcting drafts and especially Mike and Karen Lang for their editorial expertise in making sense of my notes, and finally to Constable Colin Taylor, once a young teenaged lad on a youth training scheme at Crownhill Police Station who, some years ago, looked in a builder's skip and rescued a priceless set of photographs which sparked the idea for this book.

FOREWORD

No book has been written solely about the great mutiny of 1932, an event that changed Dartmoor Prison in many ways. Buildings were destroyed where priceless files and records dating back over a hundred years were stored, yet much good came about, some say as a 'phoenix rising from the ashes'. Indeed, looking back, the events of 24th January 1932 were a milestone in the reform of Dartmoor Prison. I know from bitter experience within these granite walls that a complaint over food could be the excuse for many other issues and that a vat of watered-down porridge (the suggested cause of the mutiny) would almost certainly have been the spark to ignite a powder keg of frustration and aggression.

This book explores the real reasons behind the mutiny – the social unrest after the Great War, the new age of 'motor car bandits' confined in Dartmoor Prison and the war-worn, relentless young men who held little regard for their victims' lives.

Dartmoor National Park is a pleasant place in the summer, but from a small barred window it is unforgiving, ruthless and barren in the winter, reflecting many of the characters held in the prison – charming on the outside, but capable of bone-chilling harshness inside. The reader must remember that it was only a minority of convicts who rioted. Although many felt that they had been abandoned by society, some took great risks to save the lives of prison officers under attack, proving that even 'the most violent men in country' imprisoned in the 'cesspit of humanity' could show compassion to their fellow human beings.

If, after reading this book, you never judge all men the same and understand that even a Dartmoor convict is capable of great good then I am pleased to have been associated with it.

Mark Miller
Prisoner at H M Prison Dartmoor 2004 - 2006

MUTINY ON THE MOOR

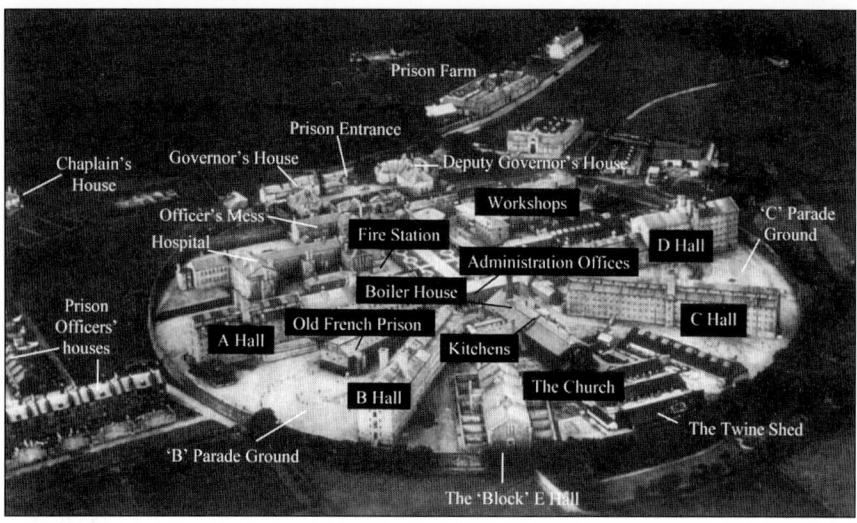

Above. An aerial view of H M Convict Prison before 1932 showing the locations of various buildings referred to in this account.

Author's collection

Below. The same view of the prison taken after 1980.

Dave Andrews

INTRODUCTION

'Dartmoor Jail was the "dustbin of the prison system"...' stated a newspaper article which gave an account of the inquiry into the riots at Dartmoor Prison, not, as you may think, following the 1932 mutiny, but 59 years later in 1991 at the conclusion of a similar episode.

H M Prison Dartmoor has always had the unenviable reputation as being one of the most famous of prisons, both in this country and throughout the world. Its reputation has been built on almost 200 years of, sometimes chequered, history. From its construction in 1809 as somewhere to incarcerate prisoners of war from our troubled past with France (and later America in 1813), to being a convict prison, a wartime settlement for conscientious objectors, a 'home' for borstal boys and now a criminal penitentiary dedicated to the rehabilitation of offenders, its

The gateway of Dartmoor Prison.
Dartmoor Prison Archives

very name conjures up images of bleak foreboding. The often misunderstood Latin words 'Parcere Subjectis', hewn into the imposing prison gateway and meaning 'Spare the Vanquished', are enough to chill the blood of any man. The article of 1991 continued thus: 'The disturbance at Dartmoor last spring led to the death of one inmate and the virtual destruction of D Wing ... ... meals were often the subject of complaint, they were frequently cold before they reached the inmates'. (It is interesting to note that the 'D Wing' of 1991 was the same building as the old B2 Hall of 1932, where much of the trouble started in the 1932 riot.)

MUTINY ON THE MOOR

The only serious differences in the two events spanning a period of over half a century were the death of one inmate and the colossal cost of the damage involved, many other aspects remaining the same. Complaints over conditions and, in particular, the food were common denominators, yet the events of 1932 go down in the annals of Dartmoor Prison history whereas the events of 1991 are almost forgotten already.

The administration block before 1932. Note the warders with Snider carbines.
Rosie Oxenham

Barely any police or prison officers, or indeed soldiers, who were involved in the frightful events of that January morning so many years ago are alive today, but the events of the 1991 riot are still fresh in the minds of those who witnessed the destruction and uncontrolled violence which was unleashed that spring day. As a constable stationed at nearby Tavistock, I was one of many police officers who were called up to Princetown, in the heart of the moor, in preparation for dealing with the human 'explosion' that was taking place within the grim walls of the formidable Dartmoor Prison – known, in 1932, as His Majesty's Convict Prison Dartmoor. Because of my keen interest in local history, the accounts and individual stories of the 1932 mutiny echoed in the ears as the events of the past seemed to be re-enacted before my very eyes. To be caught up in such an incident is terrifying indeed, irrespective of 'whose side you are on'. The officers of 1991 had modern communication, speedy vehicles, protective uniform, shields and riot helmets – all the back-up of a modern-day police force – and many, just like me, were fresh from experiences of other riots in the inner cities which so troubled the 1980s. By way of contrast officers of 1932 had no such resources, communication or support. Admittedly, some had experienced the horrors of the trenches of France, but most had their 'baptism of fire' in every respect within the prison walls that Sunday morning.

The individual stories that came out of the events of the 1932 mutiny confirm that there are, and always will be, those individuals hell-bent on anarchy and destruction; but the accounts also show beyond doubt that courageous, dedicated and committed service was performed by many. Spirit and tenacity were shown by those officers faced with the task of reclaiming the prison from the mutineers, and justice eventually won the day.

No one book has been dedicated solely to the events of that sunny morning of 24th January 1932, although many concerning the prison quite rightly refer to it. Shortly after the events of the 1991 riots I came into possession of the original photographic album containing pictures of all the buildings destroyed and damaged in 1932. It had been passed to me by a sharp-eyed young man who, at that time, was unaware of what he had saved from destruction, and had rescued the album from a builder's skip in Plymouth. Then, during the following decade, I researched the individual stories that make up the fuller picture of that notorious incident so many years ago.

Now that over 70 years have passed formerly unseen photographs and information in handwritten accounts are brought to light which paint a previously unknown picture of the events on that terrible day and the weeks leading up to it. If this story leaves you with the knowledge that there are those in the service of the Crown who are dedicated to seeing that justice will always prevail, whilst recognising that great fortitude and moral conversion can sometimes come from men who feel that they have been abandoned by society, then it is worth telling.

Simon Dell, MBE, QCB
January 2006

Left. The administration block prior to 1932, as photographed along the main driveway from the prison gates.

Rosie Oxenham

Right. Police officers with bloodhounds borrowed from a Mrs Blackesdon of Bratton Clovelly, which were used for searching for escaped convicts. The officer on horseback is from the prison pony patrol.

John Barnacott

Left. An aerial view of the prison prior to 1932.

Author's collection

1. THE CREATION OF A POWDER KEG

The years that followed the First World War saw immense social change in Great Britain, and the depression of the 1920s became a breeding ground for a different sort of criminal. The new name given to this gangster was the 'motor car bandit'. Gone were the days more suited to the felonious occupation of the footpads and 'Charlie Peaces' of the world and in came ruthless young men with little or no regard for the lives of their victims. They were aggressive and fearless; it seemed that nothing could stop them as they travelled in gangs for many miles to commit well-planned and efficiently executed crimes, and many carried guns – a rarity in the days of their predecessors. They came from a generation of young men who had spent the best part of their youthful years carrying firearms in the trenches and taking part in meticulously considered raids on the enemy. These young men with criminal tendencies were in many respects a product of their generation; their progression into crime took advantage of their experiences and pitiless attitudes to those who might dare to stop them. This, in turn, meant that the judicial authorities and the police were hard-pressed to deal with them. Indeed, once caught and incarcerated these new age criminals represented formidable captives, showing disregard for all authority and ready to attack prison warders at the first opportunity.

In contrast the 'old lags' in Dartmoor Prison, men who had spent most of their adult life behind bars, were generally compliant. They rarely spoke out of turn or assaulted the warders, but equally would not speak out against these ruthless individuals or go to the aid of a warder under attack. Of course, these differences in the conduct of the inmates in their charge became only too apparent to the prison warders, and before long it was obvious that something had to change in the establishment and everyday routine of the prison life. That change was an increase in discipline in an attempt to break the spirit of this new age convict.

From the early 1920s the discipline at Dartmoor Prison actually increased severely. It was not just the prisoners who walked a fine line of complying with the prison regulations; the warders were also in fear of their seniors and the stranglehold that they had on their own lives. Transgressing a minor regulation could mean a warder being dismissed or being moved to another prison establishment. With the job came housing and so the welfare of his family could be at stake for a minor indiscretion.

Prisoners could be sent to the punishment block for any infringement of regulation, such as talking when not permitted. The punishment block was known by a variety of names – 'The Block', 'Separate Cells' or 'E Hall' (the 'Halls' were not referred to as 'Wings' until the 1970s at Dartmoor Prison).

It was a feared place where floggings took place for seemingly minor reasons; and few men ever arrived in the Block without receiving a roughing-up for their troubles beforehand. Consequently, the relationship between warders and inmates deteriorated greatly, but staff were under great pressure to prove that they were doing their duty, and one of the quantifiable ways of showing they were not slacking was to be sending prisoners to the Block.

Convicts worked out on the open moors, in the quarry and on the prison farm; they were engaged in various hard labour activities such as wall building and stone crushing. They were poorly clothed and their meagre food ration was a source of constant complaint. After a day's hard labour they returned to their cells cold, wet and hungry only to be under constant fear of the harsh and ruthless discipline. It was therefore hardly any wonder that feelings on both sides were running high as the 1920s ended and the new decade commenced.

One significant event in the deterioration in moral at the prison was the appointment of a new governor in April 1931 to replace Major Lynden Henry Morris, who had left the prison service to take over as the Chief Constable of the local Devon Constabulary – a man who was to play a significant role in the events of the following January.

MUTINY ON THE MOOR

The new governor, Mr Stanley Norton Roberts, aged 56 years at the time of his appointment, had risen from the ranks throughout his 23 years in the service and was the first governor at Dartmoor who had started out as a prison warder. The staff at the prison had been used to 'officer types' taking charge and his appointment had not been popular. As a result, it took some time for him to obtain any respect from his staff, but eventually they regarded him as being fair and reasonable as a governor, at least to them, if not the prisoners. Unfortunately, he was most unpopular with the inmates: he was a strict disciplinarian and imposed changes which were disliked and caused tension amongst them.

Governor Roberts.
The London Illustrated News

One such significant change was in respect to the work allocated to the convicts. Until the arrival of Governor Roberts a convict could change his daily work routine after three months of doing the same job. This regular change was welcomed by the men and stopped them from becoming bored and restless, especially those facing long prison sentences. However, in the workshops it was found that this resulted in low output owing to the need to train new men every few months. As a result, the governor decided that this needed to be altered and introduced a rule that a convict could only change his job after 12 months. (In a later statement Roberts declared, "In my opinion it was necessary to slightly brighten up the discipline and to alter especially the system of the allocation of labour".) This did, in fact, lead to a greater output in the workshops, but the resentment and disquiet it caused had, perhaps, been underestimated as it led to an undercurrent of discontent amongst the inmates. Coupled with the harsh regime, which he had introduced, and the fact that he was a plain-spoken man and not one of the 'officer types', Governor Roberts became the target of hatred for many of the convicts.

By mid-1931 there were many instances when bludgeons and coshes were being discovered during cell searches. Hacksaw blades were turning up, and suspicion fell on staff who might have smuggled them into the jail, perhaps for financial reward. Many of the harder and cold-blooded convicts from other establishments were being sent to Dartmoor Prison to be closely watched and 'sorted out', but this

Sir Herbert Samuel, the Home Secretary, on a visit to the prison prior to the mutiny, along with (on his left) Colonel Turner, the Assistant Commissioner of Prisons (in the cloth cap).

The London Illustrated News

was an almost impossible task on the part of the authorities. These men of the new 'motor car bandit' age were planning and scheming. For as many cudgels and coshes that were found, half a dozen remained secreted in cells. Plans were being made for escapes, and assaults on staff as well as other inmates increased.

MUTINY ON THE MOOR

Just as 1931 drew to a close it was discovered that four convicts – Mullins, Cox, Jackson (otherwise known as Robb) and *Sparks – had indeed been planning an escape. Quite understandably these four men were kept apart in order to scupper their plans, and this led to tension. (We will hear of these four men again later as the story of the mutiny unfolds.)

To support the suspicions that an escape plan was about to be hatched was the fact that several unfamiliar motor cars were seen in the village of Princetown, where the prison was (and still is, of course) situated. For an isolated and remote community, strange faces and unknown vehicles stood out, and it was suspected that these were 'getaway' cars ready to transport would-be escapers to freedom.

*Sparks was later identified as one of the ringleaders of the mutiny. John Charles ('Ruby') Sparks, to give him his full name, was an habitual criminal who had deserted from the army in 1923. He had convictions for larceny, garage-breaking and various other crimes, and had escaped from numerous institutions, including Wandsworth and Strangeways prisons as well as Dartmoor. In 1930 he was sentenced for conspiracy, larceny and shop-breaking, and found himself again in the grim moorland prison, where he remained until 1938 – well after the mutiny. After that, at the outbreak of war in 1939, he volunteered for the army, but was soon back 'inside' again until his escape in 1940; he was then at large for 170 days, aided by the wartime blackout.

He had been given the nickname of 'Ruby' by the criminal underworld because of a burglary he had committed at the age of 16, when he broke into a Park Lane apartment belonging to a maharaja. Amongst other things, he stole a quantity of rubies, which he later gave away, believing them to be fakes! They were, in fact, worth over £40,000! His girlfriend was Lilian Goldstein, known to the local Metropolitan Police as the 'Bobbed Haired Bandit' because she drove a Mercedes motor car for Sparks when she accompanied him on 'smash and grab' raids on jewellers shops. They were the first of these modern-day 'motor car bandits'.

Feelings within the grim walls were certainly running high for many reasons – the harsh regime, the work allocations, poor food, discipline, foiled escape plans, assaults on staff, and many more besides. One of the foiled escape plans involved a convict called Jackson, who ran away from a working party but was later recaptured hanging from a hook and rope on the boundary wall. The mood in the prison then became 'electric' and everybody, inmates and staff alike, were on tenterhooks.

As the new year started a strange and silent air fell over the prison – an atmosphere which even modern-day prison officers experience and would recognise as an omen of something big about to be unleashed. Such a feeling was reported to have also hung over the prison more than half a century later in 1991, when the worse modern-day destruction to the fabric of the jail occurred.

The late Rufus Endle, a well-respected freelance journalist from Plymouth, had heard through his various 'contacts' that weapons and skeleton keys had been hidden within cells. He had also heard about the disquiet experienced amongst the inmates and that something 'big' was about to happen. This, though, was a fact strenuously denied by the authorities, but his inside information prior to the events of 24th January led to him having one of the greatest scoops of his journalistic career.

A dangerous powder keg of hatred and frustration was being primed, ready to be ignited at any moment and for any reason. The stage was set for one of the most significant events in the colourful history of the prison to be played out.

2. THE SCENE IS SET

With the disquiet amongst the inmates, and complaints being made regularly about anything and everything, it was hardly surprising that there was a protest about the state of the porridge at breakfast time on Friday, 22nd January. It seemed that an excess of water had been added to the porridge vat, as the consistency of the porridge was described as being like 'water with grains floating about in it'. Clearly the complaint was justified and something needed to be done to avert trouble.

Governor Roberts acceded that the meal was unsuitable and decided to give the order to issue an extra ration of bread (2 ounces) and

It was never ascertained why the porridge had 'failed', and whether it had been deliberately tampered with by a prisoner or even a member of staff. Whoever watered it down set in place a series of events that nobody could have predicted the severity of.

A number of former prison officers from the 1932 era as well as some from the 1960s have all commented about the possible causes of the porridge becoming contaminated with water. For decades it was the duty of the night patrol officer at 3.30 in the morning to have his half-hour break in the kitchen. When the officer arrived for his break it was his responsibility to turn on the steam to start heating the porridge vat in time for the cooks, who arrived at 6 a.m. There were four huge vats in the kitchen, each with its own steam tap and also a water inlet tap. Both taps were identical and near each other. It would have been easy to make a mistake and accidentally allow water to run into one of the vats containing the porridge. If the water had then been turned off within a few seconds no harm would have befallen the porridge, but if the water had deliberately (or accidentally) been allowed to run in for some time the entire contents of the vat would have been spoiled. Many retired officers are of the personal opinion that a night-duty officer might have deliberately allowed water to pour in and ruin the porridge. This suggestion seems not to have been investigated so is a matter of speculation, and remains as such.

potatoes (4 ounces) for dinner time, and an extra quarter of an ounce of margarine at supper time, to compensate for the lack of porridge that morning. At the time, according to a later statement made by Chief Officer Smale, it was believed that the problem had been caused by the quality of the oatmeal. (The decision to issue these extra rations was questioned in the subsequent enquiry as possibly having been ill-conceived, notwithstanding the humanitarian reasons behind it. It is a known fact among the staff of prisons that if a prisoner can get his own way by making a fuss about something then he has got the better of 'the system' and will regard this as a sign of weakness to be taken advantage of.)

Following this event, the convicts probably felt that in a relatively short period of time they had come from a situation where they were under a strict and disciplined governor to a regime where they had a governor who would seemingly give in at their slightest whim. They must also have felt that the time was right for the next move towards exerting their 'authority' within the prison walls. Whatever, that afternoon the next incident occurred, one that drew the first blood of this soon-to-be notorious weekend of bloodshed.

Prison Officer Ernest Birch was on duty as usual in the twine shed at the prison, in charge of a gang of convicts engaged in their labour. At the end of the working day he gave the usual order for the men to 'fall out' when he was immediately pounced on by one prisoner, Thomas Davis, convict number 341. Davis slashed Birch's face, on both sides of the cheeks, with a home-made knife comprising a razor blade mounted in a piece of wood; this weapon was (and still is) known as a 'chiv' in the prison world. As would be expected not one prisoner went to the help of the officer being attacked – such conduct would mean certain revenge from the underworld within the prison. However, Davis was eventually subdued and removed to the Block (E Hall) to be dealt with by the governor at a later hearing.

Ernest Birch was well liked by the staff at the prison and it was felt by the inmates that there may well be retribution meted out against them for this attack; likewise Davis was well regarded by his fellow prisoners and in their eyes he had risen in estimation for having the courage to attack a prison officer in this way. They also felt that he might well be subjected to brutality whilst in the separate cells of E Hall and this conspired together to increase tensions within the prison at a time when the explosive atmosphere could be ignited for the slightest reason. (During the course of the mutiny that followed two days later, one of the objectives of the rioting prisoners was to set Davis free by taking over E Hall.) Meanwhile, the prison assistant medical officer stitched the wounds on Officer Birch's face and it was found that the attack was so severe that the slashes had narrowly missed his jugular vein. Had this been severed little could have been done to avoid him bleeding to death!

As a precaution that evening, just after midnight Governor Roberts, who lived in the house adjacent to the prison gates, went into the prison kitchen to inspect the porridge that was being prepared for the prisoners' breakfasts later that morning – Saturday, 23rd January. After finding it to be acceptable and in good order he then went away with high hopes that the unfortunate events of the previous day, starting with the seemingly deliberately tampered-with porridge, could be put behind them and that there would be no further trouble. The governor's hopes, however, were to go unfounded, the duration of his visit to the prison kitchen – only 13 minutes (from 12.05 a.m. until 12.18 a.m.) – being a bad omen. Instead, just as breakfast was about to be served a few hours later, it was discovered that the porridge had apparently been subjected to some mischievous 'doctoring'; once again it was watery, and it was suspected that one of the prisoners working in the kitchen had added water to it to make it inedible. As a result, the prisoners then complained to Chief Officer Smale and went on to demand that they be issued with extra food before they went out on their work parties, clearly challenging the prison authority in the light of the leniency shown on the previous day. Smale, in turn, consulted with the deputy governor, who decided that 4 ounces of pressed beef be issued to the men before starting work, followed by another extra quarter of an ounce of margarine at supper time – this was literally a 'recipe' for disaster! Unfortunately, it did not have the effect that the deputy governor had hoped for. Instead, the convicts took it very badly and the tensions of the past few days mounted to boiling point after breakfast, when the prison walls echoed to the noise of rowdy prisoners protesting in their cells about the state of the food and anything else that came to mind – little did the deputy governor realise that within 24 hours the prison would be ablaze! The governor, meanwhile, decided that the regular Saturday morning meeting held in the Church of England *chapel would be delayed for an hour, until 9.30 a.m., hoping, no doubt, that things would quieten down.

*This was where a large number of prisoners would be together at one time in order to hear the general news of the week and other notices. At this time there were 440 convicts held in Dartmoor Prison so there would normally have been about 400 prisoners in the chapel after allowing for some being absent, either because they were in E Hall on punishment or in the hospital. Some of the more experienced prison warders had, it seems, warned their superiors that it was foolish to allow so many prisoners to be together in the chapel at this time, especially in view of the tensions and events of the past few days. However, it would appear that their concerns fell on deaf ears, even though it was during these types of gatherings that most of the conspiring was done: with so many prisoners together it would be almost impossible to avoid communication being made, albeit in secret, amongst them. One senior officer later went so far as to say, "Holding this meeting at this time was one of the most foolish things that has ever been done".
At this time the Church Army captain, Mr B. P. H. Ball, was the assistant to the prison chaplain and was present in the chapel at the meeting as usual; he was later ordained in 1936 and became chaplain to the prison and vicar of Princetown.

MUTINY ON THE MOOR

When it was eventually deemed safe to escort the prisoners to the chapel the governor was already there with the intention of addressing them and to explain the situation, for he felt that he might be able to placate them and avert an explosion of tension. Unfortunately, he was wrong because as soon as he reached the pulpit the trouble began again.

He started, "I want to just talk to you this morning..." and, although the unruly audience was already shouting him down, continued,

The prison chapel interior at the time of the mutiny.
Dartmoor Prison Archives

"Surely you are going to give me a hearing. I am sorry the porridge yesterday was not up to standard, and again today it is not quite as it should be. Yesterday I issued you with bread, potatoes and margarine, and today I have issued you with corned beef."

Also present at this time was the 31-year-old deputy governor, Alfred Coombe Wall Richards (one of the direct entrant 'officer types'), who

MUTINY ON THE MOOR

had held similar positions at Wandsworth and Wormwood Scrubs before arriving at Dartmoor Prison in the June of 1931. He, in fact, made an attempt to identify two convicts who started the shouting, but was unable to do so because they were so quickly joined by many of the others.

Despite the conditions the governor said what he had come to say and, after a half-hearted effort at a drowned-out and ill-considered applause on the part of a few of the prisoners, he climbed down from the pulpit and went into the vestry with the assistant to the prison chaplain, Captain Ball. The captain then asked the governor what he should do and was told, "Carry on as normal", after which the governor sped off to his office leaving him to it.

Captain Ball courageously climbed into the pulpit and announced that the planned hymn Soldiers of Christ Arise would be changed to *All people that on Earth do Dwell* – perhaps he thought better of his original choice. The prison warder organist then played the first two lines of the hymn and the convict choir stood up and started to sing, only for someone at the back to shout "Sit down, you bastards, sit down in front". At that point the choir did so and even the organist gave up, leaving the good captain to sing on along. Undeterred, he continued and after the first verse the organ started up once more and also continued until the hymn's five verses were finished. The prisoners, in the meantime, had stopped their barracking, stunned by the captain's courage in such circumstances. They then allowed him to read out the weekly news, which ended with the results of boxing and football matches – information eagerly awaited by those prisoners running the betting syndicates. Perhaps it was this information which had made them more attentive. Anyhow, Captain Ball was given a round of applause, and eventually it seemed that the tensions had eased somewhat.

After the meeting the prisoners were removed to their cells and the deputy governor congratulated Captain Ball on his tenacity and courage in averting an unpleasant scene. That evening, though, when the captain made his usual rounds and visited the prisoners in their

MUTINY ON THE MOOR

cells, he realised that, despite the inmates' jokes about his solo hymn singing in chapel earlier in the day, there was an unpleasant and foreboding atmosphere in the halls of the prison. Governor Roberts, meanwhile, had left the meeting realising that the state of affairs in the prison had reached breaking point and that had it not been for the quick thinking of Captain Ball the meeting would have denigrated into a riot. Roberts also knew that he had to do something. His staff were of the opinion that he had made a grave mistake in apologising to the prisoners over the porridge and that the convicts would take this as a sign of weakness to be exploited at their bidding.

Later, just before noon on that same day, the governor telephoned the Home Office to request permission to call upon the Devon Constabulary and the nearby Plymouth City Police to support the prison staff in the event of the situation getting out of control. He explained that tensions and feelings were running high because of the porridge situation, but made no mention of the fact that the cause of the volatile atmosphere in the prison was also due to a multitude of other factors.

A typical landing on one of the prison wings today.

Trevor James

The Home Office advised him that he was only to request police attendance and support as a last resort, but in the first instance he was to recall to duty every prison warder that was available in the hope that this show of strength would contain the situation. He did so, but as a matter of courtesy he also telephoned the Chief Constable

23

of the Devon Constabulary (his predecessor, Major Morris) as well as Mr A. K. Wilson, the Chief Constable of the Plymouth City Police, to apprise them of his situation at the prison in case he later called upon them for help with extra manpower.

It seemed that the Home Office and Prison Commissioners were so worried about the situation that they sent the Assistant Commissioner of Prisons, Colonel G. D. Turner, at once to Dartmoor Prison to 'assist and advise the governor'.

At dinner time that day further complaints were made about the standard of the food being provided due to the lack of meat, and again a decision was made by the deputy governor, as later reported by Chief Officer Smale, to issue a 'little more beef' and more potatoes to each man. This was despite his belief that there was nothing wrong with the meal.

Mr A. K. Wilson, Chief Constable of the Plymouth City Police.
The London Illustrated News

Governor Roberts now knew that his reputation and very existence was on the line; it seemed that there was nothing that could avert the inevitable from occurring. He braced himself for the events of the next day should the porridge fail again.

3. SUNDAY, 24th JANUARY 1932
THE MUTINY

It was often the case at Dartmoor Prison that if trouble was going to start then it was usually on Sunday mornings during the regular service in the Church of England chapel; this was because there were very few prison officers on duty at that location. However, on this Sunday morning trouble started even before breakfast.

The governor had arrived at the prison at 5 a.m. to check the porridge and found that the contents of one vat was perfect but those of another were watery and had clearly been tampered with again. Not surprisingly, he had then become very worried and called in as many staff as he could muster. (The number of officers on duty in the prison at the time of the mutiny is recorded as one chief officer, eight principal officers and 69 officers, giving a total of 78 staff, although many of these men were held in reserve.) Of these, two principal officers and their men were subsequently posted to the main gates and ten other officers were stationed at a nearby building to act as standbys for when the trouble, which now seemed inevitable, started. Sure enough, from 6 a.m. prisoners could be heard shouting and banging on their cell doors, the noise and disturbance being so bad that even Captain Ball, the assistant to the prison chaplain, could hear it from his home outside the prison. As a result, numerous prisoners had to be removed to E Hall to separate them, and the question then arose as to whether it would be safe to continue with the planned Sunday church service that morning, especially as the protests in one hall were starting to get out of hand – the prisoners were even singing The Red Flag.

It was then that an incident occurred that provided the spark to ignite the powder keg, which had been ready to explode for several days. In one of the halls (known as B2 – now the modern-day 'D Wing') there was a particularly noisy protest under way and there were two especially rowdy prisoners who occupied cells next to each other.

The decision was taken to remove both to E Hall, one prisoner being a known trouble-maker and the other a simple-minded man of low intelligence who would certainly not put up any fight and would go peacefully when challenged by the guards. The prisoner who was the known troublemaker, on the other hand, was in a very aggressive mood. He shouted threats to the warders and challenged them to dare to take him out by force. Even worse, as one of the prison officers, Officer Udy, entered his cell the prisoner at once drew a home-made weapon, a 'chiv' (an identical weapon to that which had injured Officer Birch so badly two days previously), and lunged at him. A violent struggle then ensued, during which the aggressive prisoner received a truncheon blow to the head and was rendered unconscious. In the meantime, the remaining prisoners on the hall could hear what was going on and it was assumed by them that it was the 'simple-minded' prisoner who had been knocked unconscious by the warders. They were beside themselves with rage and hostility.

Officer Udy, who was a senior basic-grade officer, did not receive any injuries in the incident and remained on duty, later escorting the rest of the prisoners on B2 Hall to the exercise yard, or parade ground as it was then known. (Many officers felt it foolish to allow the convicts out in large numbers for parade, but the decision for it to proceed was taken by the governor and Colonel Turner: Deputy Governor Richards was against the idea, but he was overruled.)

Before the parade actually commenced Captain Ball arrived at the prison with every intention of getting ready for the Sunday morning service. He was told that there was a risk of trouble breaking out again in the chapel, just as it had done the previous day, but seemed undaunted. The same was true after his orderly expressed concern and said to him: "If I were you, Padre, I should stick around here mostly today rather than in the halls. You'll be bound to run into trouble, even though most of us feel you did a first-rate job yesterday." Instead of taking heed of the advice, the captain responded by quoting the words 'Should such a man as I flee?' from the prophet Nehemiah and went off to inform the governor that he would start the service

MUTINY ON THE MOOR

as soon as the part-time chaplain (the vicar of Peter Tavy) had arrived. He then got ready and waited for the bells to announce the end of exercise in the parade grounds and the signal for the prisoners to make their way to the chapel for Sunday service. In the meantime, discussions took place between the governor and Colonel Turner and they decided that the service would, in fact, go ahead as planned. (This turned out to be an error of judgement in the opinion of the officers presiding over the subsequent enquiry.)

By around 9 a.m. the prisoners under the charge of Officer Udy had been removed to the B2 parade ground (this was situated between A and B Halls) and were in the midst of their exercise period. In all there were about 90 of them under the supervision of just six officers, and at this stage everything appeared to be reasonably normal. However, unbeknown to the guards many of the prisoners had gone onto the parade ground armed with coshes and home-made cudgels; the prisoners knew, of course, that it was Udy who had been involved in the supposed attack on the 'simple-minded' convict and were out for revenge against him. (Udy's very dubious and provocative presence on the parade ground was to be another matter brought into question at the enquiry.)

For a few more minutes the exercise period continued without incident but then, when the prisoners were given the order to 'Form up', their ringleader suddenly shouted "Draw your sticks. Up him boys and kick the **** out of him." He also shouted other threats directed at Udy and made it clear that he held him responsible for "knocking out the 'barmy' prisoner". However, not wishing to become involved, some of the prisoners obeyed the order to 'Form up' given by Principal Officer John Wood (the officer in charge of the parade ground), only to be met with violent outbursts from their mutinous 'colleagues', who shouted "Stand still you bastards, obey and draw your sticks".

Udy now attempted to reason with the rioting prisoners, but to no avail. Instead, the ringleaders ordered several of the other convicts to make their way to the rest of the parade grounds and to stir up their 'colleagues' to revolt against the guards there. The result was that about 50 or so rioting convicts rushed off to A, C and D parade grounds, from where, of course, other prisoners would have heard the commotion and realised by now that the revolt was under way. The remaining 'loyal' prisoners who stayed in B2 parade ground were subsequently removed to their cells, thus releasing the staff from B2 Hall to help try to regain control of a prison which was rapidly being taken over by rioting prisoners.

Within minutes the mutiny, which had commenced with the B2 Hall prisoners, had extended to C Hall parade ground. In fact, it was still only just after 9.15 a.m. when Officer Kelly, on C Hall parade, heard the commotion and saw several prisoners rush onto his parade ground to incite his convicts to break free and revolt. Many of his charges then immediately joined in and ran off the parade ground with the gathering numbers of prisoners who had united in the revolt. The focus of attention of some of the marauding prisoners was E Hall, and their intention was to storm it and release confined prisoners, including Davis who had slashed Officer Birch's face on the previous Friday. Led by a convict called Conning (wearing a stolen trilby hat), and with four others – Sparks, Kendall, Roberts and Dewhurst – included in their number, this particular mob went on to attack Warder Edward Tucker once they had forced their way into the building. However, a 'loyal' convict named James called them off and, in doing so, almost certainly saved the warder's life. (James was later dealt with leniently at the trial as the records show.)

The main ringleaders of this mutiny, as witnessed by Principal Officer Wood on the parade ground, were convicts Bullows, Conning, Garton and Moore. The fact that they came on parade armed with home-made weapons showed beyond doubt that this was a well-planned and premeditated riot, although in the circumstances it was probably not totally unexpected on the part of the prison staff.

MUTINY ON THE MOOR

The mob, meanwhile, had still succeeded in snatching Tucker's keys, so was then able to unlock the doors of the cells in E Hall and complete the 'mission' – although only after one of the ringleaders ('Ruby' Sparks) had momentarily held them off, in some act of mercy, so that the officers manning E Hall could run for their lives.

Whilst this was taking place Gate Officer Dowse, on duty at the main gates, saw what was happening as other prisoners started attacking the administration block, which housed the governor's offices. As a result, just after 9.30 a.m. he telephoned Plymouth City Police to inform them that the convicts had started a mutiny and to ask for reinforcements to be sent. He also requested that the Devon Constabulary be informed and to send help. Having done that, he then telephoned Crownhill Barracks in Plymouth, where the Eighth Infantry Brigade (which included members of the 1st Battalion of the Worcestershire Regiment) was stationed, also asking for help. In the meantime, the Chief Constable of Plymouth, Mr Archibald K. Wilson, quickly responded by telephoning Crownhill Barracks as well and was offered two companies of infantry and machine guns; plans were also set into place to muster as many Plymouth City Police officers as possible to make their way up to the prison.

The governor and Colonel Turner, along with Deputy Governor Richards, were in the governor's office in the administration block at this time, and by now their attention had also been drawn to the noise outside, which included the sound of breaking glass. Furthermore, stones suddenly came hurling through the office windows, whereupon the governor suggested calling the police, unaware that Gate Officer Dowse had already done so. Colonel Turner, however, felt that they should wait until he went outside to try to reason with the rioting prisoners. But this achieved nothing: when the colonel did venture outside he had a bowl of porridge upturned all over him, had his watch and some money stolen, and finished up locked away in a cell for his own safety after two 'loyal' convicts, Donnovan and Forrest, had dragged him away from the confrontation.

MUTINY ON THE MOOR

By now several officers had been able to make their way to the main gates, where some were issued with *Snider carbines and instructed to position themselves on the perimeter of the jail to prevent any escapes. They were told to fire only in the event of convicts scaling the walls. Meanwhile, the hard core of rampaging convicts who had made their way to the administration block now broke into the building and set light to the record office, which contained a vast quantity of priceless documentation detailing the long history of the jail as well as routine records. (This is one of the reasons why so few documentary artefacts exist in respect of the prison's history.)

Other convicts broke into the prison officers' block just inside the main gates and stole cigarettes and possessions. To do this, pickaxes and iron bars were obtained from the prison fire station, but not before convicts Saxton and Conning had wrecked the fire engine and put paid to any hopes of extinguishing the fires being lit; some of the 'loyal' prisoners did attempt to put out a few of the fires, but they, too, were set upon by the mob.

The administration block was well alight when a ladder was put up against the governor's office window and convicts broke into his office shouting that they were out to kill him. The governor and his deputy, however, managed to escape and made their way to an old building known as one of the 'French prisons', or 'Number 3 Convict Prison', where they then hid away for the duration of the mutiny. (This building was renovated in the 1940s, when it was converted to the prison's new kitchen.) They were well aware that they were prime targets and their lives would be in danger if they dared to show their faces.

*Snider carbines were rather ancient short-barrelled rifles, used for many years by warders guarding the working parties of convicts out on the open moors or in the nearby prison quarry. These weapons did not have a 'rifled' barrel as with a conventional rifle but were smooth-bored and, furthermore, because of their short barrel, were very inaccurate. This meant the likelihood of the carbines firing a fatal shot was very remote indeed.

Ladders from the damaged fire engine were taken and clearly used in efforts to escape from the prison, giving credence to the suggestion that the whole issue was about an escape attempt and not about the state of the porridge. This idea was supported by the sightings of several unfamiliar vehicles being driven around Princetown at the time, perhaps in a well-planned effort to take escapees away to freedom.

Statements made by various warders implicated the convict Ibbesson for breaking into the administration block with an iron bar, and then for throwing record files out of the window. It was reported that these papers had been set alight by convict Mason, who had then passed some of the burning files back up to Ibbesson so that he could set light to the rooms. It was also reported that two other convicts, Del-Mar and Moore, had then appeared on the scene and set light to more files in the room.

Evidence from Officer William Palmer (a one-legged prison schoolmaster) suggested that the convicts Hardy, Conning, Bullows and Hill had been responsible for throwing rocks and smashing numerous windows in the area of the administration block. At the time both he and another officer had made their way to the library, where they avoided being attacked by the mob owing to the bravery of the convict Kendall, who had displayed sympathy towards them because of Officer Palmer having only one leg. (Kendall was the brother-in-law of 'Ruby' Sparks and acquitted in the trial.) The two officers, incidentally, had been given the opportunity to leave safely before the library was set on fire.

MUTINY ON THE MOOR

Above. 'Number 3 Convict Prison', known as the 'French prison'.
Ron Joy

Below. A newspaper photograph of the prison blaze.
The Daily Mail

MUTINY ON THE MOOR

Above and below. Newspaper photographs of the prison on fire; note the armed prison officer in the lower picture standing on the roof of one of the prison buildings, keeping watch for any potential escapees.

The London Illustrated News

MUTINY ON THE MOOR

Above and below. Photographs taken during the rioting, showing the extent of the fires started by the convicts and the destruction of the administration block. The above photograph shows the B2 parade ground in the foreground, where the mutineers rioted during their exercise period, and also the 'Old French Prison' which is the smaller, solitary, building on the parade ground.

The Western Morning News

4. REINFORCEMENTS MAKE THEIR WAY

The call for assistance was hastily acted upon. The Chief Constable of the Plymouth City Police at this time was Archibald Wilson and he gave orders for every available man to be transported up to Princetown to assist in quelling the mutiny. Major Morris, the Chief Constable of the Devon Constabulary, likewise gave orders for all available men serving in the Exeter area to make their way to headquarters in Exeter and to meet up with transport whilst he sped to the prison: being the former prison governor, he, of course, had excellent personal knowledge of the complex.

Coaches were arranged and these met the Plymouth City Police officers at their headquarters at Greenbank, just off Mutley Plain. Other Devon Constabulary men were also on their way from the Torbay area, as well as more local men from the 'county' force at Tavistock and the nearby Crownhill station, which, at that time, was the divisional headquarters for Tavistock. The officer in charge of the division was Superintendent Smith of Crownhill Police Station, and it was he who made his way to assist and command the Devon contingent until their Chief Constable arrived.

Superintendent Smith pictured outside Crownhill Police Station with Sergeant Jewell.

Mrs J. Creber

One surviving description of the events of that morning is that which was typewritten by retired Detective Constable Stephen Mansfield in the 1980s. He was one of those Plymouth

MUTINY ON THE MOOR

City Police officers who had been rushed to the village in answer to the call for assistance. His unique and contemporary account is worthy of recording in full at this point in the story, even though it includes certain minor factual errors and one in particular about the church service which never actually took place on that fateful day:-

> On Sunday, 24 January, 1932 at about 10.30 a.m. a coach load of Police Officers (31 in number) from the old Plymouth Police Force, drove into the notorious penal establishment at Princetown to quell the Dartmoor Mutiny as it became known later the world over. In those days most of the Prison Officers were housed on the Western [this should read south-eastern] side of the 30ft perimeter wall, which was dangerously close to the officers' private quarters. As we entered the village we were greeted with strains of cheers and handkerchiefs were much to the fore wiping away the tears of relief at our arrival. The officers' families, mostly apron clad, were all crouched in fear outside their front doors. To them it seemed their cry for help had been heard and so, as my senses took in the situation, the human drama that began days before began to reveal itself and unfold the terrible consequences that were to follow.
>
> However, to start at the beginning. On that memorable Sunday 50 years ago, the Chief Constable of Plymouth (A K Wilson) received word of serious disturbances within the Prison. This was no rumour. The events that followed pinpointed the affair as the most serious occurrence in the history of the British Prison Service. Plymouth had opened its eyes to a sharp and gloriously sunny January morning with just a faint frostiness in the air. The Church bells of St Andrew's (the Mother Church) rang out their peals and everyone and everything was seemingly at peace with the world. How wrong we all were.
>
> Having recently become a member of the Criminal Investigation Department it was customary to report for duty on a Sunday at 9.30 a.m. From my home in the suburbs my Headquarters at the Guildhall

MUTINY ON THE MOOR

was about a 20-minute walk. In those days the police forces of this country were equipped only with a car for very senior officers and one or two motorcycle patrols. Apart from foot patrol, cycles were the only other form of transport. About ten minutes from Police Headquarters I was alerted by a motorcycle patrol and told to make all speed to HQ. He was then gone in a cloud of dust and mystery. Upon my arrival, I was bundled into a locally hired coach (then known as a chara-a-banc) and 31 officers of all ranks and the Chief Constable headed for Princetown. Not one of us knew the reason for this emergency. Rumours of mutiny over pay by the warders and other likely stories prevailed, but they proved unfounded. Only Princetown would reveal the truth so we sat back and waited. That journey of 14 miles averaged about 45 miles per hour and, by the speed standards of the day, that was some trip.

Our arrival in Princetown, as previously indicated, could have been likened to the return of a successful Welsh Rugby side heavily sedated by the pathos of the situation. Approaching the prison entrance we could see great clouds of black smoke and high shooting flames coming from within. We disembarked outside the main gate and were shepherded between the outer and inner gates. From this position we could see all. As the minutes sped by so the authentic stories of the trouble finally reached us. It would appear that for days a strong resentment had been built up by the prisoners over the quality of the food and general conditions. Cat calling, banging of utensils and refusal to co-operate continued with regular monotony. Plans for a revolt were made by the prisoners and the 24th was the deadline. Knowing that a Sunday would be a reasonably quiet day staff wise, the usual volunteers for Church were paraded and escorted accordingly – about 117 in all. The remaining 400 prisoners had no part in it as they were all securely accounted for in the prison.

During the Church Service, it was pre-arranged that prisoners seated around the Warder's look-out dias' [sic] would, at a given signal, grab their legs and in no time the five or six officers on duty were

MUTINY ON THE MOOR

hostages. The 117 prisoners then had the complete freedom of the prison and all the frustrations and feelings of the past few days were spewed out in a hate that knew no bounds. The remaining prison staff could do nothing except position about five officers around the perimeter wall with rifles to prevent any mass escape. This was the fear I referred to earlier in my story when we drove into Princetown (regarding the safety of the families). Army units stood by, but were not required. The ugly situation was somewhat relieved by the knowledge that the cell keys for the remaining 400 prisoners were safely held at the main gate offices.

Through the inner iron gates our Chief Constable tried to negotiate with the ringleaders. He was compelled to take the initiative because the Governor, Mr Roberts, could not be located. He was found later locked in an administrative office. Meanwhile, the prisoners had reduced the prison interior to a shambles. Subsequent prison riots were like a Sunday school outing by way of comparison. After failing to negotiate with the riot leaders, the Chief Constable ordered the gates to be opened and said, "In you go lads, it's them or us, so spare no mercy". That precisely was the situation and we needed no reminder of our position.

The prisoners had every weapon imaginable except firearms. I have always said, and do so again, that had they stood as one complete unit they could have slaughtered us. Breaking into the present time, for one moment, I know exactly how the lads must have felt in the Inner City Riots. 'Goody-goody' methods have to go by the board in these circumstances. Corrective methods can take place later but preservation is the first consideration. So it came about that when we made our baton charge and closed with them, they split into groups. We couldn't believe our luck and their stupidity. Twenty-five minutes or so and it was all over. Both sides suffered broken limbs, cuts and severe bruising and, except for one prisoner with a fractured skull, nothing more serious. I noticed a particular moral to this encounter, which remained with me for the remainder of my

MUTINY ON THE MOOR

Police Service. These tough guys don't mind dishing it out on the weak and defenceless, but how they squeal when they have to take it themselves.

It was now mid-afternoon. The Governor had been found unharmed and again assumed command. Every prisoner was stripped as a baby, each garment was searched and the convict placed back in a cell. During their freedom, one of the buildings they had access to was the canteen. Consequently, they were relieved of all the goodies and items like razor blades. Although having had such prolonged and unauthorised freedom, the prison regulations were carried out to the letter. Half an hour's exercise on the parade ground under the watchful eyes of prison officers and policemen. Those few moments caused me to ponder on the quote (author unknown). "Dartmoor is the cesspool of humanity". [It was actually in 1927, just five years before the mutiny, when the then Home Secretary, Sir William Joyson Hicks, visited Dartmoor Prison and called it thus.] Unfortunately, as it was, never was there a truer quote as we watched those derelicts of humanity follow each other with anti-clockwise monotony.

A meal was then served and amidst the smouldering remains of the Administrative block, the completely desecrated Church and organ and the utter annihilation of the prison itself, I consumed my dry bread and a pint of beer. My first food for that day. We all returned home to Plymouth in the same coach at 5.45 p.m. and, as I entered my home, my father was just purchasing a Special Edition of the local paper headed "Mutiny at Dartmoor". I told him to sit down and I would tell him all about it. He knew, of course, as a policeman I got into all sorts of dramatic situations but this one really made his eyes 'pop'.

(In all accounts there will inevitably be differences of interpretation as to what the person saw and considered, but Mansfield's account remains a vivid and eloquent story from the perspective of one of those police officers faced with restoring order in the prison. The 'look-out dais' to which Mansfield refers was the high chair upon which the warders sat to survey the convict congregation. His description of the distress of the prison warders' wives would be no exaggeration, for some of their homes were less than 15 feet from the walls of the prison: from the upper windows of their homes they could look down into the exercise yards and see the riot unfolding before their very eyes. There was also no security fencing on the inside perimeter of the prison walls as there is nowadays, so therefore marauding prisoners were free to go anywhere, unrestrained, within the prison. Had a convict put a ladder up to the outer wall it would have been an easy jump onto a nearby warder's house, and freedom.)

The prison on fire showing, at the bottom of the photograph, the close proximity of the officers' houses to the perimeter wall and the lack of any inner security fence.

Devon & Cornwall Constabulary Archives

Just as the police contingent was being assembled the journalist Rufus Endle was quietly enjoying a peaceful and beautiful sunny Sunday morning. During the previous night he had been aware that the police

MUTINY ON THE MOOR

in Plymouth and also the military had been put on alert in case of trouble at the prison. Nevertheless, he decided that the Sunday morning was a fine day for a round of golf at Yelverton.

Just as Rufus was driving to the golf course, blissfully unaware of what was taking place at Princetown, he was overtaken by a speeding black police car containing the Chief Constable of Plymouth City Police, 'Archie' Wilson. Rufus knew immediately that this meant something serious and took off in hot pursuit of the police vehicle, only to be overtaken shortly afterwards by a coachload of Plymouth City Police officers making their way to the prison. Something big certainly was taking place he decided, so he continued his pursuit as the two vehicles made their way up over the moors to the isolated village of Princetown.

Also on their way were members of the Plymouth Police Fire Brigade, under the command of their fire chief, Superintendent Mead, who had been alerted because of the destruction of the prison fire appliance. In any event, the local Princetown Fire Brigade could not possibly have coped alone with such enormity of buildings ablaze, so other fire engines were essential to try to save the prison once order had eventually been restored.

As was the general custom for many large incidents at that time, members of the local St John Ambulance Association accompanied the fire appliances in their ambulances in case of injuries being

Superintendent Mead.
Devon & Cornwall Constabulary Archives

41

MUTINY ON THE MOOR

sustained in the course of fire-fighting. The account written by Staff Sergeant Skinner of the Association makes interesting reading:-

> On the 24 January, 1932, The Plymouth St John Ambulance Association known as the "Plymouth and District Ambulance Service", were brought before the public eye, to an extent never seen before in the history of our service.
> On Sunday morning the 24 January, 1932 at about 11 o'clock the city fire alarm system in Plymouth rang for a grave outbreak of fire. The Central Ambulance Station at Notte Street was incorporated in this system. The first ambulance and crew left immediately behind the fire apparatus, this being the practice in Plymouth whether or not there are casualties at the fire.
> Then the ambulancemen had the unique experience of having merely to follow the fire brigade to "an unknown destination". To their surprise they went to no fire in the city, but instead were at about 45 miles per hour, soon rushing over Dartmoor. Then the information was given to the ambulance staff of a serious business.
> The Princetown Convict Establishment is situated on a desolate part of Dartmoor about 15 miles from Plymouth, and, as the Brigade and Ambulance approached the prison it was evident by the smoke and flames, also the state of the inhabitants of the little moorland town – mainly dependants of prison officers – that grim work was ahead. A large coach filled with Plymouth police officers had gone on previously, and under the command of the Chief Constable A.K. Wilson, who also is a member of the Order of St John.
> Our Ambulance took up duty near the scene of the fire which was raging in two large buildings practically unchecked as the mutineers had destroyed the fire apparatus and put the engines out of action. Then the ambulancemen reported for duty in the prison hospital, whence the wounded had been taken. There were about 80 or 90 casualties. The injuries presented themselves into about three categories.

MUTINY ON THE MOOR

1) Wounds from shotguns.
2) Contusions, bruises and some fractures sustained in the fighting.
3) Injuries, the result of falls from walls, etc.

On the very serious development of the situation a further call was put through to the Central Ambulance Station, Plymouth, and the remaining men on duty were sent to reinforce the men on scene. They took with them the comprehensive disaster equipment, which includes not only the ordinary first-aid dressings and appliances in large quantities, but oxygen reviving mechanism, breathing apparatus, smoke masks, life lines, etc.

Tentative arrangements were begun, which if the necessity arose, would have resulted in about 150 ambulance personnel being available. The staff work at the Central Station was by Mr. J Bardsley (assistant secretary of the Plymouth & District Ambulance Service). Other officers there included Lady County Officer Mrs Balrdon, who specially came from a neighbouring town to stand by, and Duty Superintendent for the day was A.R. Ponsford.

The second and larger detachment of men and transport were under the charge of Staff Sergeant Reginald Skinner, (Plymouth Central Division). He took his men to the prison hospital where their services were badly needed and most gratefully accepted. Our ambulancemen, in some instances, had to use their own dressings.

When the wounded were treated and removed, either to hospital beds or to their cells in the prison buildings, our work consisted in standing by the Fire Brigade in case of accidents during their dangerous task. The duty terminated at 10 p.m. Great respect was paid to the Plymouth Central, Mutley, and Friary Ambulance Divisions.

As a direct result of their splendid efforts, there was received "a letter" from Mr Alexander Paterson, his Majesty's Commissioner for Prisons, which read:

"May I take this opportunity of expressing the thanks of the prison commissioners and the Dartmoor Staff for all the splendid work that your organisation did on Sunday last. We were very grateful indeed to you for your timely help".

(Signed)   ALEXANDER PATERSON
From: PRISON COMMISSION, HOME OFFICE, WHITEHALL, S.W.1

Five months later a Vellum bearing an inscription of thanks from the Order of St John of Jerusalem was presented to the Plymouth and District Ambulance Service and was received by Staff – Sergeant Reginald W. Skinner; Privates Reginald Sampson (later to be Chief Ambulance Officer), Albert Drake, M. Glossack, A. Niles, P. Godes, E. Middleton, W. Macey, W. Davies, Albert Parkin (later to become Chief Ambulance Officer), Irvine Tripp, A. Phillips, and Hedley V. Miller (County Commissioner and founder of the Plymouth organisation).

As Rufus approached the village of Princetown he could see flames and smoke rising high above the prison and then realised that there was something far more serious taking place than what he had originally contemplated. The 'convoy' ahead of him, meanwhile, continued until reaching the entrance to the prison, where the officers alighted and the Chief Constable was seen to consult with prison officers at the gates. Then, shortly afterwards, a second coachload of police officers arrived, this bringing their total number up to almost 50; they were armed with truncheons, although three held pistols. (At this time there were no armed response police units as we have today. Instead, each station would have had a revolver and some bullets locked in a cupboard, to be issued to the on duty officer only in the direst of emergencies – clearly this was one such occasion.) When the reinforcements of the 1st Battalion of the Worcestershire Regiment from Crownhill Barracks arrived in their ageing lorries, loaded with infantry, rifles and two machine-guns, they were not directed into the prison; instead, they were positioned just outside to contain the perimeter wall in order to prevent escapes. One account from a soldier responsible for one of the machine-guns records that he was situated directly outside the main entrance of the prison, at the building associated with the prison water-supply reservoir. His machine-gun was placed covering the entrance of the jail and he was instructed that should a mass breakout take place then he was to 'Let them have it'. Alas, this verbal account is all that remains since he is no longer alive, but if this was the case, and there is no evidence to disprove it, the police officers were not just sent in to restore order in the prison, they were also fighting to save the lives of prisoners who would have been mown down if they had escaped. The result would have been a bloodbath equalled only by the massacre of American prisoners of war on 6th April 1815.

A copy of the *Daily Mail* report on the Dartmoor Prison mutiny.
The Daily Mail

MUTINY ON THE MOOR

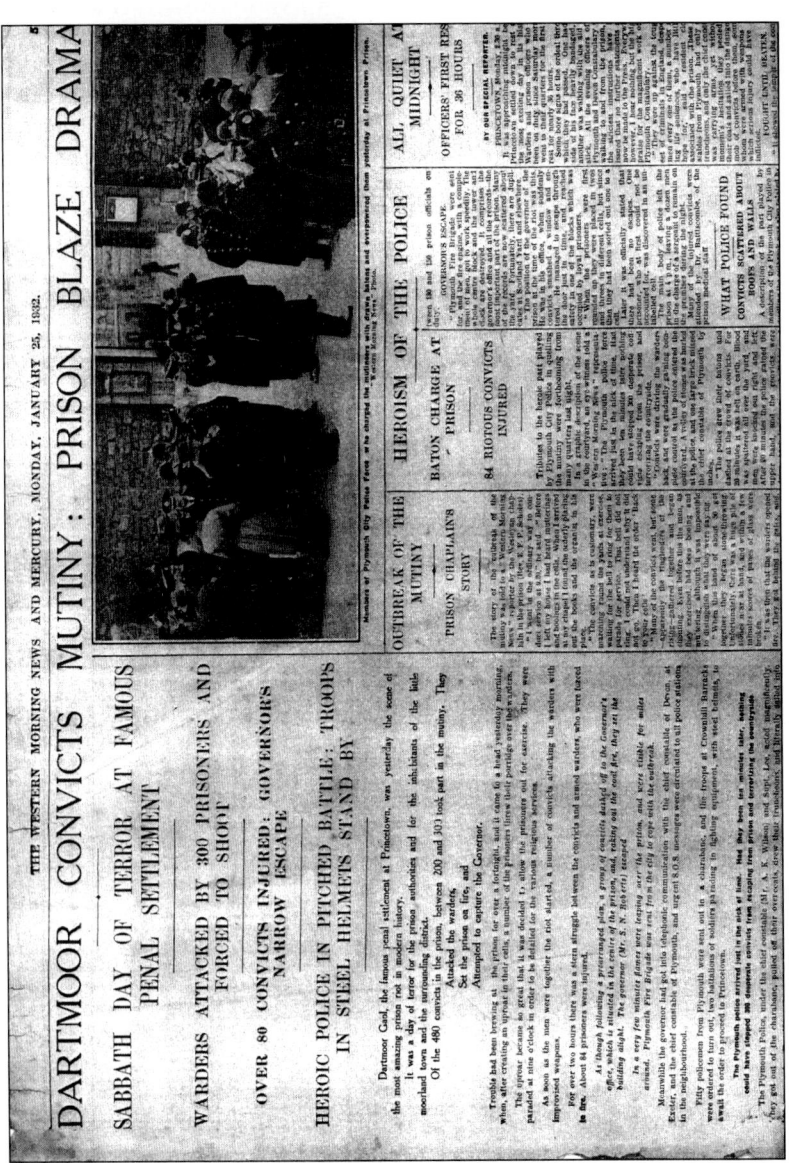

A Western Morning News account of the prison mutiny.
The Western Morning News

5. THE MUTINY CONTINUES

As the police and military reinforcements were making their way to Princetown, unaware of the severity of the situation that they were about to encounter, the prison officers struggled to 'hold their own' against the mob of prisoners hell-bent on destroying the prison.

Some of the convicts were also making a concerted attack on the main gates in an effort to effect a mass escape, even though a number of warders were now positioned on the perimeter of the jail armed with Snider carbines. During the course of the mêlée one prisoner, Gardener, was shot in the neck by Prison Warder Moss, who was sitting in a tree overlooking the twine shed; others also received bullet wounds for their trouble. One prison officer, Trask, stationed outside the jail with a carbine, reported that the top rungs of a ladder appeared over the perimeter wall of the prison, closely followed by a pair of hands and then the face of convict Ibbesson. Trask and another officer, Gordon, then fired their carbines and shot the convict, who fell back into the prison. On seeing this, other prisoners were incensed and shouted "The bastards have killed one of our men, come on boys, stop at nothing. Murder the bastards." They failed to notice, however, that Ibbesson soon picked himself up and hobbled off to the hospital. Another prisoner, Mullins, also scaled a ladder intent on escape, but when he poked his head over the perimeter wall he was met by Warder Goble with a pistol saying, "If you come

Prison officers involved in quelling the mutiny.

The Daily Sketch

down here you're for it". Mullins obviously thought better of the situation and soon disappeared within the bowels of the jail. Altogether seven prisoners were shot in circumstances such as these, but, despite many of their own men being felled and injured during this onslaught, the prison officers continued to prevent any mass escape.

In the overall confusion some prisoners also broke into the officers' quarters, where they proceeded to get drunk on spirits stolen from the building, while others forced their way into the prison band store and were making every effort to play the instruments. One of these prisoners was convict Castor, who was a member of the prison band, and it was rather noticeable later that the only musical instrument which had not been destroyed was a single cornet – the personal property of Castor! (It is interesting to note that, during the 1991 riots, prisoners also broke into the musical instrument store within the chapel and set about destroying them – how history repeats itself in many respects!) A few of the even more violent prisoners, though, were focussed on one thing only – the wholesale slaughter of the guards; they armed themselves with stolen 'weapons' from the butchery and workshops or carried bed legs with glass embedded in them and went on to attack anyone, including other prisoners, who stood in their way.

The carnage continued until the prisoners had complete control of the interior of the prison.

At one point the unfortunate Wesleyan Minister, the Revd Ernest Scholes, was chased by a group of prisoners wanting to take possession of his bunch of keys. However, he quickly made for the Church of England chapel, where his keys were reputed to have been dropped down some organ pipes to avoid their capture. He was then overpowered by a group of prisoners and was being held by the convict Del-Mar when he was rescued by Dr Richmond, the deputy medical officer, who grabbed him and rushed with him into the hospital, where they bolted the doors.

As mentioned previously, during the course of the disorder the governor and his deputy had hidden themselves away in one of the old French prison blocks, for their presence, should they have been located, would certainly have exacerbated the situation and both may well have lost their lives needlessly.

A group of prisoners broke into the boiler house intent on finding and attacking the prison officer in charge of the boiler room. The account, written by that officer after the event, illustrates the great fortitude and courage that was shown by his small team of 'loyal' convicts who, by their quick thinking, without doubt saved his life. He wrote to the subsequent enquiry explaining that a 'loyal' prisoner had ushered him into the rear of the boiler house:-

Revd Ernest Scholes, the Wesleyan Minister.
The Illustrated London News

Gentlemen,

I respectfully state for your information that on the morning of the 24.01.32 I was in charge of the Boiler House and Central Heating Plant assisted by prisoner No 464 J Jordan. When the riots started prisoner No 373 Wilson came to the Boiler House for protection, I put him employed on hiding all the fire tools and anything that might have been of use to the rioters. When I saw the mob was out of control I locked the door, and with the help of the two prisoners mentioned above, made a barricade against the inside of the door. The Boiler and Central Heating Plant was working until 15 minutes before the police charge. Then I saw from the windows, one of the prisoners who was shot from the wall being carried to the hospital. The mob was then shouting, "Kill the screws". A prisoner No… Stanley shouted in the window "For God's sake get your screw away, they are after him and it means murder". Before he could say any more they were hammering at the door. I then locked the door leading to the Central Heating Plant. No 464 J Jordan smashed the water gauge glasses and drew the fires causing the place to be filled with steam and smoke (a pre-arranged plan) by that time the mob were practically in, under cover of the steam I went to the back of the boiler with prisoner no 373 Wilson. The Boiler House was full of the mob searching for me, I heard 464 Jordan shout, "Don't touch any valves or you will blow yourselves up with it". Then the police and officers came and Jordan went for assistance, being accidentally shot in the arm during the mêlée. I then re-lit the fires put the boiler in order and started the Central Heating Plant working.

Gentlemen I should like to state that, but for the pluck and level-headedness of 464 J Jordan, I should have received serious injury, also the central heating plant would have been completely destroyed.

I Am Sirs,

Yours Respectfully

A Hicks

Temporary Stoker

(The 'loyal' convict was subsequently rewarded for his actions in having his sentence reduced.)

Whilst all this was occurring Dr Richmond, who had earlier rescued the Wesleyan Minister, was called to the main entrance of the hospital to be met with a crowd of prisoners armed with knives and staves: they were carrying a wounded prisoner, shot in the head whilst attempting to scale the perimeter walls. Undaunted, the doctor had the casualty taken inside, but even as the prisoner's wounds were being treated a chair leg with glass splinters was hurled into the hospital, injuring the medical orderly there – nobody, it seems, was immune from attack by the marauding mob of prisoners as they rampaged out of control throughout the prison on their orgy of destruction.

6. HELP ARRIVES

Dr Guy Richmond recalls in his autobiography Prison Doctor that he received a telephone call in the hospital from Archie Wilson, the Plymouth Chief Constable, who was by then at the front gates with his officers ready to enter the prison to restore order. Richmond then goes on to say...

> He asked me to go to the gatehouse and confer with him. In spite of having been told to stay in the hospital I said I would get there somehow. The hospital was fairly close to the gate but that it seemed a long way, dodging the wild and almost demented men, who were racing around like dervishes. It seemed minutes before they opened the gate to let me out. Officers had the barrels of rifles thrust through the bars, aiming down the driveway. Where, outlined by flames of the burning building, a mass of rioters had gathered. The Chief Constable asked me if I knew where the senior officials were. I told him I hadn't a clue. He said [that in view of the absence of the governor and commissioner] he would lead his men into the prison followed by the firetender from Plymouth and he warned that there would be many casualties to treat. When the gates were thrown open I watched as a solid mass of blue poured into the yards led by the Chief holding his revolver. The constables were unarmed except for their sticks.

The 'firetender from Plymouth' was under the command of Superintendent Mead and his graphic account of the actual charge is similar to that of many of the others involved:-

> When we entered the prison we found ourselves in an ambush of convicts. They had mounted the buildings and walls on either side of the main approach into the prison and were hurling bricks and stones at us. The police behaved magnificently. They hit out to the right and left with their batons and quickly overcame the resistance

of the convicts. Many of the convicts who had taken shelter on the tops of the walls inside the prison were forcibly dragged off. Other convicts escaped to the roofs of the main buildings but were hunted and captured by the police. All the convicts were then brought to the main gate, where, still under cover of the warders' guns they were searched, and tobacco, cigarettes, and other articles which they had taken from the canteen were removed.

(As already mentioned in an earlier chapter, Chief Constable Archie Wilson made valiant efforts to reason with the convicts, efforts that were met only with jeers and abuse. He then lost no time in turning to his men, drawing his revolver, and saying to them: "It's going to be them or us lads. Draw your sticks and show no mercy."
He was the first man through as the gates were thrown open, heading a charge of thirty-one police officers and six armed prison warders who were facing a formidable foe of over one hundred well-armed, rioting convicts – some of the most dangerous men in the country, who were hell-bent on killing anyone opposing them.)

Chief Constable Archie Wilson and his men of the Plymouth City Police pictured after quelling the mutiny.
The Western Morning News

MUTINY ON THE MOOR

POLICE SCENES OF CRIME PHOTOGRAPHS

The following images were taken by a local Plymouth photographer, Cyril Gill, as part of the police investigation into the riot. They are reproduced here by courtesy of the *Devon & Cornwall Constabulary* archives.

Right. The main administration block pictured from the front drive.

Left. The front of the chaplain's office, with a studio above. To the left is D Hall.

Right. The interior of the deputy governor's office.

MUTINY ON THE MOOR

Left. The interior of the governor's clerk's office, showing the single officers' quarters above.

Right. The interior of the governor's office, again showing the rooms above which had been the single officers' quarters.

Left. The interior of the record office pictured from the schoolmaster's office.

Right. The rear of the offices with the pump house behind.

Left. The Church of England chapel with two of the windows broken.

Right. The Church of England chapel showing the damage caused to the vestry door.

MUTINY ON THE MOOR

Left. The Wesleyan chapel taken from A Hall parade ground.

Right. The rear of the Wesleyan chapel taken from the front of the fire station.

Left. The Roman Catholic church entrance door with smashed windows.

MUTINY ON THE MOOR

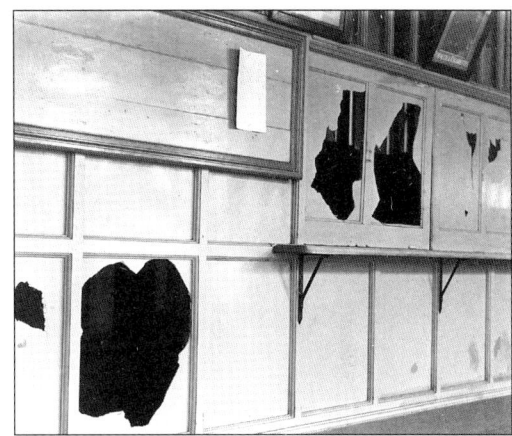

Right. An interior view of the officers' mess showing damage to the partition windows.

Left. Another interior view of the officers' mess showing damage to the windows and furniture.

Right. An exterior view of the officers' mess front door and the damage to the barred windows.

MUTINY ON THE MOOR

Left. Plymouth City Police officers, including Archie Wilson, the Chief Constable, outside the prison gates after the riot ended. The constable on the right, in the foreground, is from the Devon Constabulary.
The Western Morning News

Right. Constables of the Plymouth City Police leaving the prison.
The Western Morning News

Left. The reporters and photographers of the press mingle outside the prison to await the exit of the police who quelled the mutiny.
The Western Morning News

7. ORDER IS RESTORED

After final calls to surrender were given, but obeyed by only a handful of convicts, the charge of the thirty-eight officers began at around 10.45 a.m. Truncheons were wielded left and right, leaving convicts lying on the ground in the officers' wake. Many of the more cowardly ringleaders attempted to plead that they were actually trying to stop the rioting and joined in with the 'loyal' prisoners to avoid any well-deserved truncheon blows. The prisoners then scattered, luckily for the police, for had they stood well organised in defiance they would have outnumbered the authorities almost 4 to 1. As it happened, when the convicts divided they were easier to get under control.

One police officer met one of the ringleaders, Davis, sitting on a wall and eating a sandwich stolen from the kitchen. When asked what he was doing, the convict replied: "Eating a sandwich". "Well, here's something to put in it!", replied the police officer, felling him with a blow. Another convict was caught jumping up and down on a silver-plated euphonium. "What are you doing that for?", he was asked. "Because when the judge gave me five years he didn't sentence me to listen to the prison band", came the reply. He was then dealt with in a similar manner.

By 1 p.m. all was over with the exception of the fire-fighting efforts being carried out by the Plymouth Police Fire Brigade, whose main aim now was to save the administration block. However, after some 10 hours of fighting to bring the fire under control the ornate clock

With such little mercy being shown by the vastly outnumbered police officers, it was, perhaps, hardly surprising that within 15 minutes the mutiny had been brought to an end. After that, order was restored, the last remaining militant convicts were rounded up and the governor, along with his deputy, was able to come out of hiding in the old French prison block; Colonel Turner was also released from his 'safety cell' and joined them in taking back control of the prison.

tower and bell, nearing collapse, had to be pulled down and the rest of the building had been reduced to little more than a shell. This, in turn, also meant that valuable records going back for more than a century had been lost forever in a few frenzied hours of destruction. It can only be regarded as a miracle that nobody was killed and no prisoners had escaped.

Left. Officers of the Devon Constabulary who also attended Princetown in the aftermath of the riot, pictured with Superintendent Smith (in the coat and trilby hat) from Crownhill Police Station.
Devon & Cornwall Constabulary Archives

Right. An aerial photograph of the firefighting efforts which continued in order to dampen down the smouldering remains of the administration block.
The Western Morning News

8. THE AFTERMATH

Once order had been restored came the job of taking back control of the prison. Prisoners were stripped and searched; contraband loot and weapons were seized and convicts were either returned to their cells or removed to the hospital if their injuries warranted it, although numerous other prisoners decided not to report their injuries for fear of reprisals. Ringleaders and the main protagonists were taken to the Block for segregation.

Other police officers arrived, too late for the main attack but, nevertheless, essential in helping to reclaim overall control of the jail. Amongst their number was the Chief Constable of Devon (the previous Dartmoor Prison governor), Major Morris, who received cheery greetings from both inmates as well as staff who remembered him.

The hospital overflowed, as expected, with convicts nursing a variety of injuries needing attention. Casualty lists were drawn up: of the prisoners, twenty-three received truncheon injuries which resulted in ten of them being removed to the hospital,

An aerial photograph of the smouldering remains of the administration block.
The Western Morning News

and seven received firearm wounds, of whom four were also hospitalised. In addition, an unknown number of injuries caused by other prisoners led to two more inmates being admitted to the hospital and, as previously mentioned, scores refused to make any complaints for fear of reprisals. Dr Guy Richmond, in his later book *Prison Doctor*, recalled, 'We must have sutured up over 70 scalps that day'.

Of the officers and staff, Warder Birch was transferred to Plymouth Hospital along with four of his colleagues whose injuries necessitated treatment; twenty other officers suffered less serious injuries and carried on with their work. However, one officer was eventually invalided out of the service.

The reticence of the Home Office to 'tell all' was quite apparent in their press release on the evening of 24th January. It was limited to 217 words and stated that about 100 convicts out of 400 had broken away and that the staff were, for a time, unable to obtain control. The press release also stated that about twenty prisoners had received minor injuries, but in reality, of course, twenty-three prisoners had suffered from truncheon wounds and seven had been shot.

Alex Patterson pictured in the centre of the group.
The London Illustrated News

The senior prison commissioner, Alex Patterson, travelled overnight on the Sunday to come down to the Devon prison. The last ten miles of his tortuous journey were made on the pillion of a local newspaper boy's motorcycle, since there was no other transport available. With exhausted staff dealing with the prisoners, who by now had resumed their howling, Patterson authorised the mobilisation of the military to provide reinforcements around the prison, much to the relief of staff and families living in the grey shadow of the prison walls. As a result, the soldiers of the 1st Battalion of the Worcestershire Regiment were recalled the following day, for the Gate Book at the prison records that Lieutenants Gilmore and Bickford, along with Second Lieutenant Vaughan with 64 men, entered the prison at 9 a.m. on 25th January and remained there until 6.30 a.m. on the following morning.

Eventually daily routine settled and the long task of rebuilding or demolishing irreparable buildings took place. These, of course, included the administration block, which the Plymouth Police Fire Brigade had fought so valiantly, in vain, to save.

One little known fact about the weeks following the rioting involved the prison farm and the responsibilities for looking after the animals there and the general farm duties. Owing to the fact that so many convicts were unable to resume their work in the farm buildings, the students from Seale-Hayne Agricultural College in south Devon were brought in to care for the stock, to milk cows and to tend to the feed for horses etc. No doubt, the students regarded this distraction from their daily routine as a welcome learning experience as well as providing a valuable service to the authorities.

Prison officers carrying milk churns - usually a job performed by convicts.
The Illustrated London News

Another 'casualty' of the riot was Governor Roberts, who was now a broken man. He was subsequently moved, upon Patterson's orders, to Cardiff Prison. Major Charles Pannall, MC, DSO, who had been brought in from the Camp Hill borstal on the Isle of Wight, replaced him and went on to remain in charge at Dartmoor Prison for thirteen years, including the duration of World War Two.

MUTINY ON THE MOOR

Left. Convicts working on the demolition of the administration block.
The Daily Mail

Right and below. Prison officers, with wounds bandaged, returned to work almost immediately after the riot.
The Illustrated London News

9. THE ENQUIRY

Following the riot, the Home Secretary ordered a Commission of Enquiry to be led by Herbert du Parcq, KC, the Recorder of Bristol and a prominent figure on the 'Western Circuit' of the assizes, who would start work immediately with 14 days to complete his task. To assist him, senior officers from the Metropolitan Police (headed by Detective Chief Inspector Walter Hambrook, along with Detective Sergeant Bell) came down to Devon to undertake the exhaustive research required and to take the many hundreds of pages of

Herbert du Parcq.
The Illustrated London News

statements from those involved. Recalling his briefing at the time, Hambrook wrote: 'I had already received a most vivid impression of the magnitude and gravity of this startling event, which was without precedent in English crime. On the previous evening I had been to a West End cinema, and amongst the news pictures shown were photographs taken from an aeroplane of the prison building belching forth flames and huge columns of smoke. The area of destruction was so great that it all seemed too bad to be true.' Hambrook knew a good deal of the prisoners and notorious gangsters, gunmen and 'motor car bandits' at Dartmoor.

(The riot was, at that time, the second worst in the history of the prison, only being eclipsed by the mutiny 117 years previously involving American prisoners of war, who had had their uprising quelled by an armed militia; this had resulted in seven deaths, sixty seriously injured and many more slightly hurt.)

Du Parcq went to great lengths to uncover the reasons for the mutiny and the events surrounding it. His findings can only be described as startling. Over a period of some three months prior to the mutiny numerous instances of skeleton keys and hacksaw blades being found on prisoners had come to light. Du Parcq stated that in his opinion it was "almost inevitable that some members of the prison staff had smuggled them in". Du Parcq later went on to say, "In my opinion, the Governor made a serious mistake in addressing the prisoners in the terms which he used. His actions were well meant, but in my view such conciliatory and even apologetic language was likely to be interpreted by many of the prisoners as a sign of weakness and timidity."

It was not just the senior ranks that he slated. Officer Udy's actions in appearing on the parade ground also came under fire because of the inflammatory effect it had on the prisoners. Du Parcq regarded it as 'ill-advised', but did go on to commend the officers and police as well as the 'loyal' prisoners who helped save many warders. Inevitably one man came in for personal criticism, and it was unsurprisingly Governor Roberts. "The Governor has been, in my opinion", stated du Parcq, "an excellent administrator, and I believe him to have been just in his dealings with the prisoners. I think that a man of exceptionally strong character might have been able to quell the growing disorder by the force of his personality. It is, I hope, not a severe criticism of Mr Roberts to say that he does not have this rare gift."

Upon answering questions in the House of Commons, the Home Secretary, Sir Herbert Samuel, took the opportunity to make a brief statement welcoming the report. He promised that proceedings would follow based upon the evidence that was presented, and that the conduct of those prisoners who had helped the authorities 'should be suitably recognised'. He mentioned that damage had been assessed at £3,000 and went on to state that the future of Dartmoor Prison was under review and that it would, perhaps, not be there much longer. (This was not the first, nor was it to be the last, time that the future of this most famous, or infamous, of prisons would be discussed in Parliament.)

The actions taken following du Parcq's report were speedy, and preparations began for the inevitable prosecutions of the ringleaders and those involved in the mutiny.

10. THE TRIAL

In little more than a month in the jail Detective Chief Inspector Hambrook had obtained statements from everyone involved and his findings were sent to the Director of Public Prosecutions, who decided to charge thirty-four of the convicts.

Two of their number, Thomas Davis and David Brown, were taken before the magistrates at Tavistock Guildhall, charged with wounding with intent to cause grievous bodily harm to Officers Birch and Udy. Their appearance at Tavistock Court, so the local press declared on 4th March, caused Tavistock to be 'Drawn into a vortex of excitement'. This somewhat

Davis and Brown arriving at Tavistock Court.

David German

eloquent overstatement was perhaps pardonable, for rumours had abounded for days that convicts from Dartmoor Prison would be appearing at the court on charges which had come about as a result of the great mutiny a few weeks previously. Moreover, the rumours had been confirmed in the national press on the previous day, and by 10 a.m. a group of onlookers had gathered at the court.

At 10.30 a.m. a fleet of motorcars and police motorcycles appeared and were subsequently seen to swing into the guildhall car park outside the police station and court buildings. The two prisoners were then ushered into the courtroom and presented before the magistrates at 11.15 a.m.: less than 15 minutes later the hearing had been concluded and the case against both was adjourned.

Shortly afterwards both men were driven away to the applause of a cheering crowd, Brown smiling and Davis waving his hat obligingly. They had, nevertheless, both been charged with the attacks on the

Tavistock Guildhall entrance at the time of the trial.
John Barnacott

warders, and one week later thirty-two other prisoners were also to find themselves being charged with offences, including riot, damage, arson and robbery. It was decided, however, that to hold the preliminary proceedings for all of the offenders at Tavistock Court would stretch the resources of local police and transport operators. Instead, the magistrates went to the prison, where the cases were later formally opened and adjourned to be heard at a special court that was to be held at the local Duchy Hall in Princetown village, which was being equipped for the subsequent trials.

The hearings for Davis and Brown, however, were resumed at Tavistock Guildhall court, where they were committed to stand trial at the hastily erected and temporary assize court at Princetown. (Brown was later found not guilty of the assault, but Davis subsequently received an extra 12 years imprisonment for his troubles.)

The preliminary hearing at Princetown's Duchy Hall was presided over by Colonel Marwood Tucker, along with other magistrates who included the local builder, Mr Halfyard, JP.

A large wooden dock surrounded by iron rails had been erected for the accommodation of the prisoners and the officers guarding them, whilst the

Mr Halfyard, JP leaving the prison.
Rosie Oxenham

magistrates sat on chairs on the stage. The hearing occupied nine days. Each morning the thirty-two convicts, all in their own clothes, were driven down from the prison along the main street to the Duchy Hall with a strong police escort. Officers had been drafted in from all over the county. One such officer was George Roper. He recalled that his Newton Abbot landlady gave him fried mackerel at 6 a.m. each morning prior to making his way up to Princetown – without realising the consequences: instead, she failed to take into account that her lodger, and fellow officers, travelled in the old, hard-tyred Force removal lorry (normally used to remove officers between country beat stations) and that the route consisted mainly of winding lanes over Dartmoor via Moretonhampstead and Postbridge. Only once did the fried mackerel 'survive' the tortuous journey! George also recalled that he had been given a revolver because of the fear that an attempt might be made to free some of the prisoners. He had never handled a firearm before that time and because he was dressed in a coat and peaked cap, in an effort to provide 'undercover security' at the proceedings, felt somewhat ill at ease.

Princetown village, showing the location of the assize court at the Duchy Hall.

Aerofilms Ltd

Someone else who gave a later account rather strangely recalled that a large Japanese lantern hung from the ceiling, a bizarre remnant

MUTINY ON THE MOOR

Left. Officers of the Devon Constabulary arriving for the trial.
Devon & Cornwall Constabulary Archives

Right. Officers escort the lorry containing the mutineers on their way to the Duchy Hall.
Devon & Cornwall Constabulary Archives

Left. The arrival of the mutineers at the Duchy Hall. The three-wheeled vehicle in the foreground is one of the earliest motor patrol vehicles of the Devon Constabulary, stationed at Roborough Police Station.
Devon & Cornwall Constabulary Archives

from a previous festive occasion in the village. Although the prisoners were manacled to the iron rail when in the dock, they were given excellent treatment. They had 'elevenses' as well as a special lunch at the hall, followed by a cigarette. Ironically, the convicts at the nearby prison had constructed the wooden dock and its iron rails.

The front of the Duchy Hall.
Devon & Cornwall Constabulary Archives

Following the preliminary hearing in the presence of the magistrates, one of the prisoners was discharged, but the remaining thirty-one were committed to appear before the assizes. This, it was decided, would also be held at the Duchy Hall in the village.

The court was the same, except that the prisoners had chairs and sat in tiers with a number in front of each of them for ease of identification, and a large plan of the prison hung where all could see it.

Constable George Roper, in the cloth cap, seen standing on the steps of the Duchy Hall.
Devon & Cornwall Constabulary Archives

The subsequent trial was preceded by the customary church service in the local church, built by French and American prisoners over a hundred years previously. The approach path to the church was lined with local Girl Guides and Wolf Cubs from the village.

The first hearing was of the grand jury, a system still in use in America, but abolished here

Left. The procession of assize officials entering Princetown churchyard, led by Major Morris, the Chief Constable of the Devon Constabulary.
Ron Joy

in 1933. This initial court made sure that there was a case to answer before the main assizes heard the prosecution and defence evidence, and was a safeguard for an obviously innocent person.

'True Bills' were returned against all of the accused and the dates for the assizes were set.

Right. Following the church service, the procession leaves the church watched by the gathering crowds.
Ron Joy

The assize court was presided over by the Right Honourable, Justice William Viscount Finlay, KBE, one of the justices of the King's Bench Division of the High Court of Justice. He was accompanied by the High Sheriff of Devon (Samuel Manning Manning-Kidd Esq.) and the High Sheriff's Under-Sheriff (Henry Ford Esq.) along with his chaplain. The Solicitor General – Sir F. Boyd Merriman, KC, MP – and two other King's Councils prosecuted, while six barristers, including one KC, were for the defence. The clerk of the assize was John William St. Lawrence Leslie Esq. (The judge had a retiring room, but there was insufficient space for the barristers, who made do with the school across the road in which to robe themselves.)

The precise form of the indictment read: 'That they on January 24, 1932 at Lydford [this was the local parish] in the county of Devon, being riotously and tumultuously assembled together to the disturbance of the peace, feloniously, unlawfully, and with force, did demolish, pull down, or destroy a building devoted to public use, or erected or maintained by public contribution, contrary to Section 11 of the Malicious Damage Act 1861'.

It might be reasonable to assume that the trial was a serious and boring affair. On the contrary, there were numerous incidents which brought some well-needed opportunities of humour to the occasion. One shortish convict, named Jackson, decided to conduct his own defence along with the skill and panache of a long-standing barrister, complete with pince-nez spectacles, which he took off and waved at the witnesses whom he was cross-examining. He started, once the governor had given his evidence, "I am in a position, my Lord, which is unique in that for the first time since I have been a prisoner I can question officials and demand an answer". He then began his cross-examination on administrative matters and was afforded polite replies. His first setback came when he asked why he had been transferred to another working party. The governor replied, "I had good reason to believe that you were going to try to escape".

"How did you know that?", asked the convict.

"I think my theory was correct because you actually made an attempt on January 18", replied the governor.

His real downfall as a barrister, however, came when questioning another officer.

"Can you tell me why you woke me up from being unconscious by bashing me on the thigh?", he asked.

When the officer replied "I did no such thing", the convict retorted "What? No such thing? Why, I saw you".

Everyone laughed and the judge remarked that, "There is a rather obvious comment but I will not make it".

He may have had his moment of limelight, but the convict was eventually given an extra six years of penal servitude to run consecutive to his existing sentence.

Another rather amusing incident came when the local vicar was called to give a character testimony for one of the accused. He spoke highly of the man, but upon the counsel's last question, "So you know of nothing against him?", the clergyman hesitated. The counsel then feared he might say something detrimental to his client so he interrupted by saying, "Oh, don't bother", but the judge instructed the question to be answered.

The vicar added, "Well, he once played an execrable solo on the euphonium".

Another convict, Davis this time, added to his defence and said that "I was passing the boiler house and I saw that there were only two panes of glass left so I broke them, to make the windows symmetrical. I found some food and the biggest policeman who asked me what I was doing approached me. I said I was having a sandwich and he hit me on the head with his truncheon, saying 'now make a ham sandwich out of that', there I was dancing with tears in my eyes."

One prisoner produced a battered silver cornet as evidence of how he had been victimised and said, "I had hoped to earn a living with this when I got out". He also stated that he had been a loyalist and had attempted to restore order by blowing 'fall in', but had then decided that 'defaulters' might be better understood only for the police to have come charging into the prison: "Look at my cornet now", he complained.

It took the jury five hours to reach their verdict. Twenty-three convicts were found guilty of various offences, including riotous assembly and malicious damage, but ten were found not guilty. Some of those ten whose sentences had expired were released immediately. The others received sentences ranging from six months, to twelve years for the man convicted of injuring Officer Birch. In all, Mr Justice Finlay passed sentences on 13th May 1932 totalling a few months short of 100 years.

Those convicts dealt with by the assize court, along with their sentences, are as follows:-
William H. Beadles and David Brown were both found not guilty and released from the court to continue to serve their existing sentences.
Thomas Bullows was found guilty and sentenced to 8 years penal servitude to be served consecutive to his existing period of imprisonment. (This meant that this period was added to his existing sentence.)
Harry Burgess was found guilty and sentenced to 3 years penal servitude to be served consecutive to his existing period of imprisonment.

Officers carrying exhibits to the trial, including ropes and grappling irons planned to be used to effect escapes.
Devon & Cornwall Constabulary Archives

Anthony Castor was found not guilty and released from the court to continue to serve his existing sentence.
Joseph Conning was found guilty and sentenced to 10 years penal servitude to be served consecutive to his existing period of imprisonment.
Patrick Cosgrove was found guilty and sentenced to 20 months penal servitude to be served consecutive to his existing period of imprisonment.
Thomas Davis, one of the mutiny ringleaders, was found guilty and sentenced to 12 years penal servitude to be served consecutive to his existing period of imprisonment for his assault on Warder Birch.
James Del-Mar was found guilty and sentenced to 18 months penal servitude to be served consecutive to his existing period of imprisonment.
Thomas E. Dewhurst was found guilty and sentenced to 3 years penal

servitude to be served consecutive to his existing period of imprisonment.

William Gardener pleaded guilty to a minor charge of damage and was dealt with leniently by being released from the court to continue to serve his existing sentence, but mutineer George Garton was found guilty and sentenced to 3 years penal servitude to be served consecutive to his existing period of imprisonment.

Alfred Greenhow, Herbert Hardy, Alfred Hart and Albert H. Hill were all found not guilty and released from the court to continue to serve their existing sentences.

James Horn was found guilty and sentenced to 21 months penal servitude to be served consecutive to his existing period of imprisonment.

One of the longer sentences was handed out to James Ibbeson, another ringleader, who was shot down from the twine shed roof during the disturbances. He was found guilty and sentenced to 10 years penal servitude to be served consecutive to his existing period of imprisonment.

John Jackson (otherwise Robb), the convict who defended himself, was found guilty and sentenced to 6 years penal servitude to be served consecutive to his existing period of imprisonment.

Edward James, being one of the 'loyal' prisoners, was found guilty but recommended to leniency for going to the aid of an officer being attacked: he was sentenced to just 18 months penal servitude to be served consecutive to his existing period of imprisonment. Another 'loyal' prisoner was Patrick Kavanagh, who was also found guilty but recommended to leniency for going to the aid of an officer being attacked: he was sentenced to just 15 months penal servitude to be served consecutive to his existing period of imprisonment.

Victor Kendall was found not guilty and released from the court to continue to serve his existing sentence.

William Mason was found guilty and sentenced to 8 years penal servitude to be served consecutive to his existing period of imprisonment, along with both Walter F. Moore and Alexander Muir, who were both sentenced to 3 years penal servitude to be served consecutive to their existing periods of imprisonment.

John Mullings was found not guilty and released from the court to continue to serve his existing sentence.

Frederick Roberts was found guilty and sentenced to 3 years penal servitude to be served consecutive to his existing period of imprisonment.

Charles A. Saxton was found not guilty and released from the court to continue to serve his existing sentence.

Frederick Smith was found guilty and sentenced to 8 years penal servitude to be served consecutive to his existing period of imprisonment.

The infamous Charles J. ('Ruby') Sparks and his compatriot Harry Stoddard were both found guilty and sentenced to 4 years penal servitude, again to be served consecutive to their existing periods of imprisonment.

Sidney Tappenham, a 'loyal' convict, was found guilty but 'strongly' recommended to leniency for going to the aid of an officer being attacked and was sentenced to a mere 6 months penal servitude to be served consecutive to his existing period of imprisonment.

Joseph Taylor was found guilty and sentenced to 3 years penal servitude to be served, like everyone else, consecutive to his existing period of imprisonment.

POSTSCRIPT

Several of the 'loyal' prisoners who had helped prevent serious injury, or even death, to warders were rewarded with remission and reduction in their sentences. This meant that some convicts were released immediately.

The driver of the coach, Mr C. Webb of the Western National Omnibus Company, who took the Plymouth policemen so speedily to the prison that morning, was not forgotten. His service was rewarded with a special presentation made by the Dartmoor Prison Officers' Club: it took the form of a silver replica revolver, representing a fast and exciting drive at speeds of up to 45 mph made to the prison – a speed virtually unheard of in those days!

The mutiny on 24th January 1932 might, unwittingly, have been one of the most progressive events to take place at the prison. As a result of the rioting, conditions for prisoners were closely scrutinised, work allocations were reviewed, wages were paid for work, and penal systems were updated. Perhaps the overall benefits enjoyed by successive inmates who followed those 'motor car bandits' of yesteryear might well be regarded as the phoenix rising from the ashes.

Left. Prison officers on parade in the presence of the Assistant Commissioner of Prisons, Colonel Turner.

Rob Hare

BIBLIOGRAPHY

Dartmoor Prison by Rufus Endle (Bossiney Books, 1979)
Dartmoor Prison – A Complete Illustrated History Volume II by Ron Joy
(Halsgrove, 2002)
Dartmoor Prisoner of War Depot and Convict Jail by Trevor James (Orchard Publishing, 2002)
Inside Dartmoor by Tom Tullett (Frederick Muller Ltd, 1965)
Parliamentary Report of Mr Herbert du Parcq, KC (February 1932)
Prison Doctor by Dr Guy Richmond (Nunaga Publishing, Canada, 1975)
Prison Was My Parish by The Revd Baden P. H. Ball (William Heinemann Ltd, 1956)
Statements taken from prison and police officers, along with prison staff and other witnesses, held in the Devon & Cornwall Constabulary archives relating to the 1932 mutiny.
Tavistock's Yesterdays – Volume 1 by Gerry Woodcock (G. Woodcock, 1985)
The Assize Report (25th April 1932)
The Daily Mail Newspaper reports of 1932 and since relating to the 1932 mutiny
The London Illustrated News (30th January 1932)
The Prison On The Moor by Robert Sanderson (Privately published, c1970)
The Sunday Independent (24th January 1982)
The Western Evening Herald (now the Evening Herald) – various articles relating to the 1932 mutiny
The Western Morning News – various articles relating to the 1932 mutiny

THE AUTHOR

Simon Dell came to Bideford in North Devon as a schoolboy with a burning desire – like many boys of that age – to be a policeman. Later, whilst still attending school, he developed a passion for Dartmoor and then decided that not only did he want to become a policeman, but to become a policeman on Dartmoor.

Eventually, after leaving school in 1975, he joined the Devon and Cornwall Constabulary and served at a number of stations before realising his ambition in 1980 by being posted to Tavistock, where he was to remain as the local community policeman for 16 years. He was a member of the Dartmoor Rescue Group for almost 20 years, being awarded the MBE in 1997 for services to Dartmoor Rescue and the community. Later, in 2002, he received the Queen's Commendation for Bravery for saving a father and son from a burning building. He has written a number of books on the subject of policing history and has appeared on television and radio, speaking on that subject. He still lives in Tavistock with his wife Shirley, son Matthew and daughter Laura, and is in great demand throughout Devon and Cornwall for talks and lectures on the history of policing. He still finds time, however, to enjoy walking on the moors, either with his border collie Patch or with visitors to the area as a recently qualified Dartmoor National Park guide.